YOUR psychic pathway TO NEW BEGINNINGS

YOUR psychic pathway TO NEW BEGINNINGS

A SIMPLE GUIDE TO GREAT ADVENTURES

Sonia Choquette, Ph.D.

Clarkson Potter/Publishers

NEW YORK

Published by Clarkson Potter/Publishers, New York, New York.
Member of the Crown Publishing Group, a division of Random House, Inc.
www.randomhouse.com

CLARKSON N. POTTER is a trademark and POTTER and colophon are
registered trademarks of Random House, Inc.

Material in this book was originally published in *The Psychic Pathway*,
Your Heart's Desire, and *True Balance*.

Printed in the United States of America

Design by Jane Treuhaft

Library of Congress Cataloging-in-Publication Data
Choquette, Sonia.
Your psychic pathway to new beginnings / by Sonia Choquette.—1st ed.
1. Parapsychology.   2. Spiritual life—Miscellanea.   I. Title.
BF1041 .C48   2002
133.8—dc21   2001050035

ISBN 0-609-61013-9

10 9 8 7 6 5 4 3 2 1

First Edition

Your desire for a fresh start
is worth celebrating.
It means that your soul is inviting you
to return to your authentic self.
Listen to this desire and pay attention.
Follow this desire, even if it's
not clear where it will lead. It will open
the way to your heart.

You can achieve your heart's desire for a new beginning by entering the psychic pathway. This means becoming receptive to spiritual assistance. It is a sacred pathway that emphasizes your creative purpose and your spiritual growth. It is the pathway of the extraordinary life.

When you walk the psychic pathway,
you look at life differently
and respond to it differently. You know
that you are being helped
with each experience you face,
no matter how difficult.

The Chinese have a saying:

The way it begins is the way it ends.

Begin your new project by affirming:
"I am a spiritual being protected by angels,
helped by guides,
and infinitely loved and supported
by the Universe."

Awaken Your Intuition

Entering the psychic pathway will give you a fresh perspective on old issues and will lead you to new conclusions. You may encounter resistance from others as you take steps to bring new responses into your life. Therefore, you should first commit to discretion and self-protection, including excellent self-care—a healthy diet, adequate sleep, exercise, and recreation—for the duration of your journey into a new life.

Allowing your psychic voice to guide you will make it easier to create your new intentions. To awaken this voice, you must tell your subconscious mind that you intend to be psychic. The best way to communicate this intention to your subconscious mind is through gentle repetitive suggestions. Here are four affirmations that will help you awaken your intuition:

1. *I am now open to psychic guidance in my life.*

2. *I will expect psychic guidance to help me on my way.*

3. *I will trust all psychic guidance that I receive.*

4. *I will act on my psychic guidance without hesitation.*

New beginnings are possible when you see yourself as a *natural receiver* of psychic guidance. When you intentionally focus on being open to guidance, you position yourself to receive all the help from the Universe that you possibly can. In fact, you are being psychically helped and influenced all the time. It happens with every "coincidence" you experience. It happens when you think of someone only to have that person call the same day, or when you spontaneously change your plans for no reason and as a result intercept a very important opportunity.

Imagine that your awareness is a natural radio receiver designed to tune in to communication from your Higher Self at all times. Establish this intention every day: "I am open to my intuition." Being open to guidance is like turning your radio on.

By creating this mind-set, you allow subtle, supportive influences to enter your awareness and help you along the way.

Ask yourself:

Am I open to psychic help?

Am I open to guidance?

Am I willing to receive help in creating a new life?

You Are a
Natural Receiver

Be open to receiving psychic guidance
every day. Take this first step to enter the
psychic pathway and begin to benefit right
now. It will allow the Universe—including
your angels, your guides, your Higher Self,
and Divine Spirit—to assist you.
Don't continue to do things the old way,
the hard way. Do them the *psychic* way!

Be even more bold, more intentional, in your desire to have the Universe help you start anew. Once you are open to guidance, begin to *expect* it in your life. To your old way of thinking this may seem presumptuous, but once you realize that you are a natural spiritual receiver, it makes perfect sense to be psychic. You are designed to be psychic. It's natural! When you expect to receive psychic communication, you turn the dial of your awareness to a clear band of communication with your Higher Self. Your anticipation of intuitive guidance will ease you along the path to an exciting new life.

When you decide to be guided by your intuition, you place your full attention, both conscious and subconscious, directly onto your Higher Self. This decision shifts the power away from other people who are trying to run your life and places it in the hands of the Divine. You become a person who responds to life rather than one who reacts to it. This expectation of psychic guidance realigns you with Divine Spirit and the Universe at all times and attracts everything you need to succeed.

Trust Your Intuition

Expand your power even more by trusting what your Higher Self conveys to you. Trusting your intuitive feelings is often a challenge, because they cannot be immediately confirmed. You may not want to trust your feelings because you don't want to hear what they are telling you. Even so, making this decision to trust opens up a whole new way of life and spares you from repeating the patterns and mistakes of the past. When you trust your intuition, you listen to the broadcast of your Higher Self. This angelic psychic band will bring extraordinary gifts into your life.

Psychic guidance is Divine Spirit's gift
to you. Embrace this gift. Accept that
your intuition is there to help you.
It will guide you, teach you, inspire you,
lead you, and support you . . . if you
let it. This loving and beautiful force is
gentle and will not interfere with you
in any way. Intuition is a sacred gift,
one you can choose to accept.

Pay attention to your psychic sense.
It will put you in touch with your
authentic self and help you become
who you want to be in the world. And,
even better, it will show you how
to express soulfulness in your life.
Trust your intuition!

Walking the psychic pathway takes courage. It takes courage to let go of the ego-centric messages that say you are made up of only body and mind and that your worth is defined by the opinions of others. Walking the psychic pathway escorts you out of the land of the old and invites you to recognize that you are a beautiful soul who is protected, loved, and guided every step along your path.

Are you willing to approach your goal
in this new way?

Ask yourself:

Am I open to allowing my intuition to help me?

Can I expect that my intuition will be available to me as I need it?

Am I willing to listen to my intuition?

Am I willing to ask for guidance in advance?

Am I willing to have my life become easier?

true intuition,

the natural voice of your Higher Self, seeks only to make your life better. You can trust it to guide you and help you in every way. Be willing to give up your old, fixed perceptions and beliefs. Be flexible and open to redirecting yourself midstream if your Higher Self suggests that you do so. Trusting your Higher Self will change the way you are in the world. It may feel difficult, but what you experience will only be relief.

Acting Anew

Imagine that you are on an expedition in a foreign land. You don't know the terrain very well and have a limited time in which to achieve your goal. Would you welcome the advice of an expert who unexpectedly volunteered to show you the most beautiful way to experience the territory and the most efficient way to accomplish your goal? Now imagine this: You are actually given that opportunity whenever you trust your Higher Self! Your experience, if you heed this guidance, will verify that it is indeed trustworthy.

Do something different: Act on your intuitive guidance! Acting on your intuition is the leap of faith that will propel you forward into the world of the extraordinary. Every time you decide to act on your intuition, you release yourself from the limited power of your ego and place the power of your life into the hands of your soul. By acting on your intuition you allow your life to be directed by a Divine source instead of your fears. When you follow your psychic sense, you enter a brand-new world, one that works to assist you in every possible way.

BE OPEN! EXPECT! TRUST! ACT!

These four decisions shift you into the extraordinary life. Life becomes a spontaneous flow when it is carried by the beauty of your Higher Self. If you choose to live life on the psychic pathway, you experience immediate peace and inner security.

Are you willing to live on the psychic pathway?

How has your inner voice guided you today?

How has your intuition helped you
in your new goal or project?

Have you danced with your soul yet?

Would you refuse the counsel of a master builder if you were constructing a house? Would you dismiss the help of an extraordinary healer if you were sick? Would you ignore the help of an incredible artist if you wanted to create something wonderful, especially if the advice were not only free but also accurate and helpful? Probably not. And yet it somehow seems reasonable to ignore the advice of your Higher Self, which is offered with love to help you achieve your heart's desire in the most creative, efficient, and graceful way. Allow yourself to accept such a gift. Say yes to your intuition.

Quiet Your Mind

Once you agree to be guided by your
intuition, the next step is to clear away
the outdated and unwanted influences
around you. You cannot reach out
for something new until you let go
of the old. It's time to make space
for healing energies to enter your life.
If you want to be guided by your Higher
Self, you have to quiet your mind.
And the way to do that is to
learn to meditate.

Are you willing to meditate?

meditation

is quite simply the art of relaxing your body and
quieting your mind. Training your mind to be
still is like training a puppy to sit. The mind likes
to jump around and needs to be told many times
in a firm but friendly tone to sit still. Meditation
is learning to still your thoughts for about fifteen
minutes. When you quiet your mind, you break
up old mental patterns, open your awareness,
and allow your soul to speak to you.

BRE<small>A</small>THE!

Begin meditating by concentrating
on your breath. Start by taking in a slow, deep
breath right now. Notice how much you can
expand your awareness by taking in a single deep
breath and then exhaling.
This simple act stretches the boundaries of your
world a little further than you are accustomed
to and creates room for something new.
Next, inhale to the count of four.
Hold to the count of four. Exhale to the count of
four. Then inhale to the count of four again, hold
to the count of four, and so on.
Continue until you arrive at a comfortable and
natural rhythm. You can make this exercise even
easier by listening to Baroque music
as you meditate. Its even tempo will synchronize
your breathing and help create the quiet
you desire. Enjoy meditating for about fifteen
minutes, then go about your day.

Meditating will make your new goals much easier to attain. After only one week of meditating you will begin to feel the benefits. Try it and see for yourself. Be practical. Choose a time each day that will accommodate your schedule. Find a quiet place. You may have to overcome stubborn conditioning that suggests that self-care is selfish. It isn't. Self-care is loving. It will heal you. And it will open you to love others instead of being needy and manipulative. When you feel peaceful and guided, your life will unfold in a whole new way. You will attract positive people and situations, and life will take on a balanced and inspired quality.

Through meditating you learn to
distinguish the voice of your Higher Self
from other voices in your mind.
The voice of intuition is subtle,
consistent, and calming. And this voice
will lead you to new beginnings.
Listen to it and you will always
feel satisfied.

Meditate every day as a gift
to yourself!

Don't Censor

Consider everything your Higher Self conveys to you as meaningful when awakening your intuition. Don't discount anything. Pay attention to each unusual, weird, funny, coincidental, bizarre, surprising, odd—indeed, psychic—notion or feeling that occurs to you. Don't censor certain feelings because you think they aren't important enough. Every psychic impulse, however trivial, counts. Have *fun* and notice just how much the Universe is trying to help you in every way.

Ask yourself:

How has my Higher Self helped me this week
to achieve my new goals?

What gifts have I received?

Am I starting to notice just how much fun it is to allow
the Universe to be my partner?

Am I enjoying this whole new way of life?

Taking Responsibility

Many of us are raised to believe that we can't trust ourselves and must seek authorities outside of ourselves for guidance. This old way of life sets us up for failure. When you awaken your intuition, you turn toward your own integrity and away from such psychic sabotage. Instead, your intuition points you in the direction of true mentors. Your heart's desire becomes possible when you start to take responsibility for your choices in life.

As you move toward your new goals, you will be asked to stand apart from others and to commit to what is important to you. Now is the time for you to decide to be a self-directed person, one who is led by spiritual guidance, not fear.

Your intuition is a gift, but to fully experience this gift, you must take responsibility for it. You should realize that it is not something others may necessarily support. You must be willing to walk through the gate of self-direction by yourself. Once through, you'll find others like yourself, but as you approach such a liberated life you will definitely feel alone. The signpost leading into the world of the extraordinary reads "Enter only if you are willing to take full responsibility for yourself." If you choose to begin your new life in this way, you will be met with miracles, magic, and the companionship of amazing and powerful helpers.

Avoid unnecessary drama as you move into your new life. Don't try to convert anyone to your changed point of view. Using your intuition means you can operate in the world differently, but you must use this channel effectively. Start off easily, in small, nonthreatening ways. As you develop confidence in your intuition, gradually expand into more difficult arenas. Ask your Higher Self to help you in every possible way to succeed in your new goals. The Universe wants to help you. Let it.

Reinvent yourself!
Draw your self-esteem from your
spiritual nature, not from
appearances or the opinions of others.
Hold your own counsel. Don't advertise
your liberation. Let your successes
speak for you.

AN INVITATION TO JOY

Joy is a landmark of the psychic pathway to new beginnings. Witness the myriad blessings pouring upon you with every subtle twist, every magical moment, every thought, impulse, notion, or bright idea that comes your way each day. And guess what? It only gets better from here.

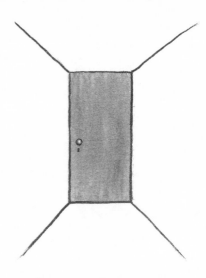

Life on the psychic pathway
is exciting. It brings new
opportunities and perspectives
directly to your doorstep. It invites
creativity, support, and genius.
Moment by magical moment,
it seeks only to create the life
you really want.

When you awaken spiritually and honor your intuition, you take a huge step toward creating joy in your life. True psychic guidance will not only protect and heal you but will bring joy to everyone you interact with as well.

Release Yourself

To create something new, you must release the past. You can't create new conditions if you don't relinquish old ones. Consider the negative feelings you may hold toward those who have hurt you. Observe your life and all its conditions: They are simply the path your soul chose to walk. The more complex and difficult your life has been, the more opportunity for your soul's growth. The best way to release the past is to forgive all that has transpired in the past. Forgive yourself as well as any other person who has hurt you.

Forgiveness and acceptance are often difficult concepts because they are confused with condoning abuse or with being passive.

Forgiveness and acceptance are neither weak nor passive acts. They are acts of great courage!

When you forgive, your healing begins.

when you forgive,

you free yourself from the shackles of the past and bring yourself fully into the moment. Being fully in the moment enables you to create a new experience. Forgiveness is a great act of personal empowerment. It frees you from others and allows you to create the new life you want.

Forgiving the Past

Begin by making a list of those who have hurt you.

_____ hurt me by _____.

_____ hurt me by _____.

_____ hurt me by _____.

_____ hurt me by _____.

_____ hurt me by _____.

_____ hurt me by _____.

_____ hurt me by _____.

_____ hurt me by _____.

When you are finished, sit in a comfortable chair. With your list in your hand, say out loud to each person:

_____, I forgive you for _____.
Thank you for teaching me _____.

If you cannot forgive someone at this time, be patient and ask your Higher Self to help you. Go back to that person at a later time and try again.

old rule

I am a mortal being full of sin,
not good, not worthy.

new rule

I am a spiritual being, a child of
Divine Spirit, inherently precious
and guided at every moment.

As you release yourself from the past, you will experience a gradual lightening of your soul. You are entering a life of spiritual peace and creative expression, in which you are a victor instead of a victim or a martyr. You can stop living by the old limitations and create a set of new possibilities. As you start to live according to that integrity, your new rules will evolve naturally.

Eliminate the Unnecessary

Just as it's important to clear the past, it's also important to clear the path if you want to introduce a new experience. If your life is disorganized or filled with lots of unfinished business, chances are you'll miss the most obvious, let alone the more subtle, whispers of your soul.

get
organized!

Disorganization is an energy leak. Look at your physical surroundings and notice whether or not they reflect order, balance, and commitment. The more order you have on the outside, the more order you can have on the inside. It's time to let go of the inessential. Purge the unnecessary! Eliminate all the outdated, useless stuff that is cluttering your home, your time, your life. If something no longer serves you, donate it back to the Universe. If it's useless, toss it out. Simplify. Lighten up. Make room for the new.

Ask
yourself:

What do I care about?

What is the most important thing in my life right now?

What am I willing to commit to?

How can I organize my life around these goals?

TRAVEL LIGHTLY

Modern life is demanding, hectic, and intense at best, but if you are sloppy and inattentive in your daily activities, you'll always be out of step with the Universe. You won't be able to move on to the new. A disorganized life is a life of stagnation, frustration, and drama. By clearing the way, you can transform this stuck energy into inspiration, creativity, movement, and new opportunity. *Do it!*

Recognize what is tugging on your attention because of neglect and clean it up so your soul can guide you onward. If you are entering a new path of spirit, you have to travel lightly. Ask yourself whether you are holding on to:

Unnecessary baggage from the past

Unfinished business in the present

Self-sabotaging fears about the future

Let go of unnecessary baggage from the past. Take care of unfinished business in the present. See your fears about the future for what they are—unreal.

What baggage from the past
must you let go of?

What unfinished business is
holding you back?

What fears are dragging you down?

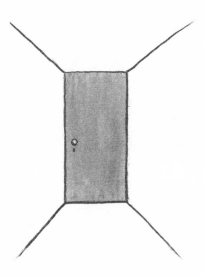

Often we say, "I want a change, but
I'm afraid I'll make a mistake."
Being afraid is normal when it comes
to trying something new. Don't wait
for your fear to go away.
Simply accept it as part of being human.

Lead from your soul—not from fear.
Leading from fear is like driving a car
with the emergency brake on:
It's painful.
Leading from intuition is like being
driven by a chauffeur in a Rolls-Royce.

letting go

does not come easily. It takes practice to let go of the old and reach for something new. Today, practice letting go of fear and listening to your heart. Pay attention to what your heart tells you. Check in with it often.

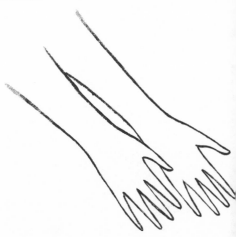

Where Is Your Focus?

Being too much in a hurry will keep you from noticing what supports your new goals. Take time to notice the world around you. Pay attention to what is going on *now*. Keep a pace that allows you to rest, meditate, have fun, and listen to your inner wisdom. That is the pathway to your heart's desire.

One way to avoid becoming distracted from your new goals is to stop asking others for their input, unless it is absolutely necessary to have it. Stop soliciting others' opinions and start asking your Higher Self for guidance. Remember, you can experience true peace of mind only when you follow *your* spirit, *your* guidance, *your* heart. Countless opinions from others will only make it more difficult for you to hear your higher counsel. Let your rule be "I'll only ask for input if the person I'm asking is wiser, happier, and more balanced than I am." Otherwise, do something completely new and ask your Higher Self instead!

Try This!

Create a wish list of the things you want to experience in your life but aren't right now. Work on the list every day for seven days. On the first day, write down twenty wishes. On the second day, pare those twenty wishes down to twelve. On the third day, reduce the list to nine wishes. On the fourth day, write down seven wishes. On the fifth day, cut it down to five. On the sixth day, prune the list to three wishes. On the seventh day, write down your three remaining wishes, those that have made the cut.

1. I wish _____.

2. I wish _____.

3. I wish _____.

These are your three true heart's desires. Tape them to a mirror, or place them where you can see them throughout the day. Stay focused on what is important to you now and remain faithful to supporting these goals in your life.

No matter what you want to create, the Universe wants to help. But it will not work harder than you do in bringing about your goals. It can't, because that would override your greatest gift—your free will. Once you determine your intention, however, the Universe joins in. As you move toward your dreams, the Universe will move toward you. Your Higher Self can help, but it won't intrude. Its influence is subtle, gentle, and noninvasive. It can only be offered if you ask for it. Invite your Higher Self to help you.

Ask yourself:

Am I meditating?

Am I forgiving those who have hurt me?

Am I clearing the path?

Am I identifying my true goals?

Am I listening to my Higher Self rather than asking the opinions of others?

Am I asking the Universe for help?

The more you realize how powerful you are as a spiritual being, the more doors will open up to you. One way to see this truth more readily is to stop considering everything from an emotional point of view. Not everything in life is personal—many things just *are*. If you observe conditions and people with objectivity, you will gain insight into what to do.

Try not to take the behavior of those around you so personally. Tell yourself, "It's not all about me!"

As you release yourself from the past and clear the way for new beginnings, life starts to take on wonder and excitement. Notice the beauty of being in the moment. Slow down, breathe, and pay attention to the miraculous world you live in today. Use all of your senses and ask:

What do I see?

What do I hear?

What do I smell?

What do I feel?

Where am I now?

Where do I want to go next?

The Energy of Others

Be aware of the world around you, including the energy of others. The more you notice, the better informed you'll be, and the better your decisions will be. When dealing with people, study them. Listen to what they are saying and focus on what they mean. When interacting with others, take a deep breath and notice how their energy affects you physically, emotionally, and spiritually.

Do you feel supported?

✳

Are you being heard?

✳

Are you in harmony with this person, or does this person have a negative effect on you?

Pay attention. Don't ignore anything. And let your own experience guide you.

If you have a positive experience, be open. If you feel drained or upset, step away if possible. Don't let this person drag you down. Your awareness will allow you to make choices that support your spirit and guide you to your goal.

Once you are alert to how people affect you, a whole new set of choices is available to you. When you learn to observe and not absorb others' negativity, you can remain faithful to what is important to you, instead of being thrown off course.

GETTING GROUNDED

As you move toward your new goals, people around you may react negatively. Change is scary for everyone, and as you change, others may try to stop you. Send them love, but protect yourself from any harmful interference. See yourself surrounded by a golden light that deflects all negativity and fear and allows only loving, positive, supportive energy to influence you.

If you are aware of how people affect you, you can keep them from doing so in a negative way by getting grounded. Grounding is a technique that calmly drains you of excess energy, thus keeping your perceptions clear, your emotions balanced, your body relaxed, and your mind focused on what is important to you.

The best method of grounding is so obvious you will not believe it: Touch the ground. That's right, simply put your hands into or onto the earth, channeling your energy back into the ground. When you feel overwhelmed, go outside. Play in the garden. Take a walk. Lean against a tree. Run around the block. Pick up a rock and hold it for a while. Do anything that will get you out of your head, out of your emotions. Channel your excess upset energy back into the ground and feel the relief.

More useful ways to ground yourself:

Exercise.

Cook.

Give yourself a foot massage.

Work with clay.

Bake bread.

Clean a closet.

Fold the laundry.

Lie on the ground.

Look at the stars.

Play sports.

Dance to your favorite music.

Drum on anything.

Keeping yourself grounded greatly enhances your success in your new endeavors. You have more energy, your mood is more optimistic, and you are open and aware. This is the perfect state for receiving guidance from your Higher Self. Being bogged down with other people's negative energy is like looking through a dirty windshield during an electrical storm. In such a state you cannot remain true to your path.

Another Grounding Exercise

Sit comfortably in a chair and remove
your shoes and socks.

Flex your ankles and feet until they feel
loose and relaxed.

Then, one at a time, place a foot in your lap
and give yourself a foot massage.

Pay attention to the ankle, the toes,
the arch, and even the calf.

Use peppermint foot lotion to enhance
the experience.

Notice how relaxed and grounded you begin to
feel while doing this. The more you massage, the
more centered you become. Five minutes will
work miracles whenever you are anxious, worried,
overextended, or fatigued and need a boost.

How often should you ground yourself? Do it as often as necessary. Do it all the time. Do it until it becomes second nature. Do it so often that you become used to being grounded as a natural state. A grounded state is a peaceful and effective state. A grounded state is a healing state. It keeps you open to new solutions, possibilities, and opportunities. It keeps you from falling into anyone else's negative energy trap. Being grounded keeps you moving forward, toward what you really want in life.

imagine it

Activate new beginnings through your imagination. By using your imagination, you shift your focus away from the sensory world of appearances and place it into the creative world of possibilities, solutions, and ideas. Your imagination is the magic carpet ride to your new hopes and dreams. Use your imagination to ask for guidance whenever you need it. Use your imagination to ask for direction. Use your imagination to ask for inspiration. Use your imagination to lead you to your heart's desire. If you can't imagine it, you can't create it. Imagination is not only the source of your psychic ability but also the source of *all* your ability.

One of the best ways to entice your imagination to lead you to answers is to play a game I call "I wonder. . . ." Every time you say to yourself, "I wonder . . . ," you summon your inner genius and invite it to shed light in dark or unknown corners. This makes it much easier for you to explore new territory.

I wonder . . .

Who's on the phone

Which elevator will arrive first

Where I put my car keys

How best to finish this project

What he or she really means

What I want to be when I grow up

What my purpose in life is

What will make me really happy

Try This!

Listening to your inner voice is an art that takes practice. Work on listening to your inner voice by first simply *listening*. Just for today, when someone speaks to you, give him or her your full and interested attention. And before you speak, listen to your heart and give it your full and interested attention. Doing this will open all kinds of new avenues, both to others and to your spirit.

Ask yourself:

Am I becoming aware of the difference between positive energy and negative energy?

Can I tell when I am being led to right circumstances or being warned to avoid wrong ones?

Am I paying attention to the subtle differences in vibration that alert me to opportunity or caution me against unpleasant situations?

What Is Practical?

We often worry that following our intuition isn't "practical," that it's reckless and irresponsible, and that following it could lead to terrible mistakes. Actually, nothing could be further from the truth. Not only is your intuition practical, it's common sense of the highest order. Following it saves you time, keeps you from taking the wrong path, improves your health, connects you to supportive people, and leads you to your true purpose in life. In fact, it's only through your intuition that you will experience peace of mind. Given all that, it's highly impractical not to listen to it.

Just for today,
resign from the "woulda,
coulda, shoulda" club of missed
opportunity. Your intuition is there to
help you. Let it work for you instead
of your working against it.

be flexible

The more flexible you are, the more your Higher Self can guide you to your new goals. And be physical about it: Get out of your head. Dance as much as you can. Stretch! Bend! Twist!

To create something new, you must introduce new energy and information into your life. Learn three new things today, big or small, to support your next goal or your new adventure.

What are they?

Remember

I f you want to move toward your dreams, don't
be attached to your fears. Don't burden yourself with useless notions, secondhand opinions,
or "reality" as other people see it. If you follow
your heart and listen to your intuition, you will
receive synchronicity and grace along the way.

I Am

The words "I am . . ." are very powerful
metaphysical words. Whenever you say
"I am . . ." you make a spiritual
proclamation—you declare who you are and
who you want to be to the Universe,
to others, and to yourself—and the Universe
agrees and is compelled to make it true for
you. That's why it is very damaging
to proclaim unpleasant things, such as "I am
unhappy," "I am broke," "I am sick," "I am fat,"
or "I am unlovable." Statements like these
absolutely attract undesirable conditions.
This week, use the power mantra "I am . . ."
to create the exact conditions
you want in your life.

I am healthy.

I am balanced.

I am happily employed.

I am loved and lovable.

I am beautiful.

I am a prosperous and creative being.

I am joyful, lighthearted, and
blessed in every way.

Ask yourself:

Am I grounding myself?

Am I noticing how people affect me?

Have I created a list of my important goals?

Do I wonder?

Have I proclaimed "I am . . ."?

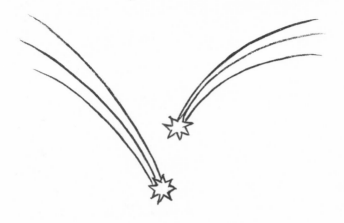

YOUR SPIRITUAL GUIDES

You have spiritual helpers called guides who are here to help you achieve your goal. They inspire you, give you guidance, offer solutions to problems, and attract your attention to opportunity. You have many different guides, and each one is devoted to helping you create the best possible life you can imagine.

You have:

Angels—to protect you

Healers—to keep you strong

Helpers—to guide you in new projects

*Teachers—to encourage you to
grow in spirit*

Joy guides—to make you laugh

*Master guides—to lead you to your
purpose in life*

Be aware of your guides. Have conversations with them.
Give them names. Get to know them!

If you want your guides to help you, simply *ask*! They can't help you unless you allow them to. When you ask for assistance, you give them permission to guide you to your spiritual awakening. Get in the habit of asking for guidance and help all the time. When you agree to be helped by your guides, you are actually helping them. You are also helping the planet. As you achieve more balance, you contribute more equilibrium to the earth.

The miracle that takes place when you follow your heart is that the benefit doesn't stop with you. Every life you touch will also be helped. The loving vibration that comes from listening to your intuition is infectious. It is calming. It is grounding. It is healing. It is inspiring. It attracts great success. When you are guided, peaceful, and happy, you grant others permission to be the same. The benefits flow out like ripples on the water.

Become a Bearer of Light

As you continue to follow the psychic pathway to creating your dreams, you'll soon realize that you are becoming a different kind of person, an *extraordinary* person. Life gets easier as you shift your emphasis toward your Higher Self and away from your fears. When you listen to your inner voice, you increase your chances for personal happiness. The more you agree to be helped, the more you help the planet. If you are spiritually peaceful, you can touch other people's lives in a positive way, and the healing effect increases. The more light you receive from the spiritual plane, the more light you radiate! You are leaving the land of the wounded and becoming a bearer of light, a true healer in this world.

Following your desire to begin anew will definitely be a healing experience. Ask your Higher Self to help you in this adventure. Approach your changes with a sense of humor and playfulness. Notice how generous and creative the Universe is in supporting your dream. Don't worry about how you are going to succeed. You don't have to know. Just be willing to allow yourself to succeed. That's the hardest part.

Listen to your Higher Self above
everything else. It will naturally guide
you to what it is you really need for
change and serenity. When you walk
the psychic pathway, you begin your
spiritual healing. You will recover your
childlike joy. You will be able to love
yourself in a deep and profound way.
You will start to feel how
magnificent you really are. And
you will be on the path
to new beginnings.

Finally, don't forget to say thank you
for all the love and support
you receive.